All That Remains

All That Remains

John Tesarsch

PUNCHER & WATTMANN

First published in 2024
Published by Puncher & Wattmann
PO Box 279
Waratah NSW 2298

info@puncherandwattmann.com

**NATIONAL
LIBRARY**
OF AUSTRALIA

A catologue record for this book is available from The National Library of Australia.

ISBN   9781923099357

Cover design by Miranda Douglas

Printed by Lightning Source International

For Dinusha, Oscar and Sylvie

Contents

The Other End of the Telescope

Endeavour

Afterwards

Coda

Die Vögelein schweigen im Walde.
Warte nur, balde
Ruhest du auch.
Goethe

The Other End Of The Telescope

Snapshots

I have read that more photos are taken now,
every minute,
than in the entire nineteenth century.
Just think of it: all those grim portraits
of General Sherman and Sitting Bull,
of Florence Nightingale and Tchaikovsky
and, closer to home, of Ned Kelly and his gang
and the bearded fathers of federation,
now hopelessly outnumbered
by selfie-stick happy snaps.
What, then, will endure when our descendants
pick through our remains — what will they find
to represent the spirit of our age?
Your photo, of that new pair of shoes,
or mine, of last night's chicken casserole?

Diagnosis

Nothing had prepared me for the moment
when my doctor called, apologised
for the intrusion, said this was about my test
results and could not wait. He told me to sit down
in a kindly uncle's voice and I did
exactly what he said. My life balanced
on the end of a pin, about to fall
in any direction; my breath caught
as though snagged on barbed wire.
For some time, I gazed at mundane things
as though they were museum exhibits
framed exquisitely behind polished glass:
a pile of empty pizza cartons;
rotting leaves on the driveway; even
muddy footprints on the porch. This, then,
was the moment that my life had always
been hurtling towards. I tried to catch
the slippery details of forthcoming
scans and appointments, and found that
I could only concentrate if I looked
at it all from a clinician's viewpoint,
or else accepted that I was already an inpatient
with a numbered wristband warning nurses
about my unusual allergies. Even then,
I was distracted by the childhood memory
of that night I had to leave the carnival
before riding the Ferris wheel,
never to return.

Anthology

If there is such a thing as immortality
then, even for the greatest, it may attach
only to a handful of lines.
Decades of labour are boiled away,
leaving only broth, easily digested,
tasting of what might have been
but is now lost.

Abstruse, lengthy works do not fit neatly
into the volume and must be discarded,
so Larkin will always condemn parents,
Auden will forever stop the clocks
and Hopkins will only praise dappled things;
one day, Dickinson may only ever talk of hope,
with feathers

Would they rail against the editors, insist
that their work should not be represented
only by five-finger exercises –
much as The Children's Bach was never
intended for the recital hall –
that instead they would prefer
oblivion?

But we must all be anthologised,
our lives compressed into brief
soundbites; so at your wake, your friends
might only declare you good company,
and on my headstone, there may only be
space for loved ones to say
rest in peace.

Second Chance

For most of us, there is no road to Damascus.
Granted, I was struck by lightning
and found myself in a hospital bed,
kept alive only by the mysteries of science,
and I resolved, like the King of Nineveh,
that if I survived I would mend my ways:
wear sackcloth, give away assets,
find meaning in random acts of kindness.

The day I was discharged, small wonders
I had never much cared for were invested
with miraculous qualities:
the rustling of autumn leaves,
the shadows cast by afternoon sunbeams,
even the satisfying crunch of gravel underfoot:
surely, nothing could ever be the same again.

But, somehow, I was corrupted.
I cannot recall the precise moment
when I thudded back to earth, bruised
like Newton's apple: it may have been
the evening I cursed the neighbour's dog
for keeping me awake, or the morning
I complained when I was overcharged
by the supermarket cashier. No matter,
I am now back to normal, fretting
about my tax return.

On Reading Aesop

Those who believe that everything is relative
should read Aesop to a child.

Historians are divided
on whether he lived and, if so,
whether he was a Thracian slave
or a princely adviser, although most believe
that he is as fictional as his stories.

Still, this much is certain: when a fable ends,
my daughter blinks, and smiles, as she discerns
the moral glistening with eternal gold dust.
Suddenly, I remember the feeling when
I first read these simple words and, somehow,
Aesop reached inside me, plucked a string
that caused me to resonate with the shimmering
overtones of a well-tuned guitar.

For example, take the fox and the stork:
in real life, she has never seen those creatures,
they do not live anywhere near our suburb,
yet she laughs as the fox serves dinner
on shallow plates, and when the stork
returns the favour with tall pitchers,
because she knows these rogues —
they sit next to her at school.

Listening to Wagner

It isn't like eating ice cream,
when the only harm is self-inflicted,
or like dropping plastic in organic waste,
when there is actual, measurable harm,
nor even like watching my mother dance to
Highway to Hell at my wedding.

I know that he was revered by madmen,
and I am vaguely aware that he was
a misanthrope who published hateful
propaganda, though I haven't read it,
so for my research I am content
to rely on Wikipedia.

As I adjust my headphones,
I wonder if I should listen
to his operas, then I hear the Tristan chord
and settle back in my armchair; still,
much like that chord, my disquiet remains,
and it never reaches consonance.

Magic Flute

They sing about beauty and wisdom
with utter sincerity,
but when the curtain falls
they rush off to their after-party
and leave behind their costumes
like discarded sock puppets,
while my sleep is disturbed by
their aphoristic burrs.

A Quiet Moment

I try not to ask for miracles,
no matter how tempted. If a friend
is sick, I accept that it won't make any
difference to ask that he is cured.
How could it, when countless prayers
have been offered replete with entreaties
to end wars, and floods, and famines,
to no avail? Yet perhaps that is
the point of it all, to know of those
calamities and accept that the course of
history has never been altered
by someone standing alone in a
field, waiting for sunset, giving only
thanks, and asking only for faith.

False Gods

They are not gods, the false gods:
they do not force me onto bended knee
and demand loyalty, or give commands,
let alone expect to be obeyed. If I have
no need for them, they are content to be
boxed up in the attic, gathering dust until
I want them back.

They are not gods, the false gods:
they are poor replicas, built with cheap materials,
and do not even pretend to be genuine.
If I asked, they would admit they are false;
they would relish the question, wink at me
with endearing collusion, and offer
boundless favour.

Memoir of the Golden Calf

I didn't want it to happen,
but the old fellow wandered off into the mist
and the others were at a loss for what to do.
Some of them settled down to sleep,
while others, bored by the fitful trek
on an endless plain under blazing sun,
had lengthy theological debates
until they devised their plan:
a plan that served no purpose
other than to fill those uneventful hours.

I watched as they melted their goblets,
earrings, coins and tinderboxes,
to reconfigure my eternal atoms
into a flattering form.
Then they grovelled in the dirt before me
while I tried to bellow through those locked lips,
to bellow: 'Wait! Don't you understand?
This won't change anything between us
and you won't get any closer to the truth.
Besides, when the old man returns, he will curse you
and dash me against the rocks.'

They didn't hear me and their worship continued:
but don't blame me, I was only a calf at the time.

Another Way of Looking at a Blackbird

It should give me cause for hope,
give all of us hope — lawyers, doctors,
accountants, engineers, pathologists,
mail clerks and dental technicians —
even though our right brains have been
encircled by the left, that an
insurance executive still had the time
and the inclination to find thirteen
ways to look at a blackbird.

Ode to a German Automobile

Even though it is caused by volatile
organic compounds and has been linked
to nausea, migraines and even cancer,
she finds it intoxicating,
that new-car smell.

She sits behind the wheel as the dealer
explains the interactive dashboard,
climate control, rear-vision camera,
semi-autonomous parallel parking,
then the myriad safety features: airbags,
lane-keeping assistance, and especially
blind-spot warning.

Her world is suffused with new-car smell;
hopefully it isn't unduly toxic: still,
how can she make a rational decision
when in thrall to this perfume?

The dealer isn't just selling luxury, but also
lifestyle, and tells her this will be an ideal
companion, that she can afford this,
that she has earned this, that it is truly
a thing of beauty, designed by the world's
finest automotive engineers,
and for modest payment she can upgrade
to electronic seats, leather upholstery,
even a moonroof.

She can also upgrade the sound system
from eight to twelve loudspeakers,
but as she turns the dial and checks the quality,
she hears Schubert's Trout Quintet:
it reminds her of better days
and she has to escape.

Endeavour

The Search for the Perfect Metaphor

While others play the stockmarket
or build their property portfolios,
I sit at my desk, staring out the window,
searching for an invisible thread
to loop together random ideas.

When I finally grasp that thread
and tether my thoughts with a makeshift knot,
I am consumed with wonder and delight,
although my act is of no more consequence
than if I had solved a cryptic crossword.
After all, there is no reason to suspect
that this invisible thread explains
the mysteries of the universe
any better than quantum mechanics.

These Days

These days, surely he would write film scores:
not for him a life of penury, beholden
to artless princes, teaching gormless brats
and waiting for lucrative commissions;
not for him the unrelenting labour
of writing intricate symphonies
and sonatas, or performing keyboard wonders
for witless nobles when, instead, he can
dash off simple tunes for blockbusters
and live in a mansion with ocean views.
Surely the composer of The Magic Flute,
and Figaro, would dream up memorable themes
that rival the shark motif in Jaws,
even Darth Vader's march, worthy of ring tones
and keeping the financiers satisfied.
He would have a sportscar and health insurance,
and Constanze wouldn't have to worry
about whether they can afford college fees.
True, there may come a time when he asks for
study leave, or a lengthy sabbatical,
so that he can explore ideas that are
far too speculative for Boxing Day movies
and that keep him awake at night. Of course,
with no one else like him in Hollywood,
the executives would begrudgingly agree,
while hoping that he soon returns.
Yet their real concern would be that he is lost
to advertising, not just for the money
but also the camaraderie. After all,
Keats and Shelley are now writing great
commercials.

Rockstar

There were two of him, always two.
Even when he strutted across stage
wailing those banshee lyrics, flaunting
that bicep tattoo with its snake and dagger;
even when he sang about dirty deeds
and breaking out of jail;
even when he was drunk or high:
there were always two.

The other can be seen in black-and-white,
with a leprechaun beard and lumberjack shirt,
playing the recorder, or a weird
contraption that brings to mind a bassoon,
or warbling with an operatic voice:
a hippie from the Adelaide Hills
smiling in a psychedelic trance,
part of a fraternity who never cracked
the national top forty.

If the hippie had found chart success, would we
have seen the rockstar and his ripped denim?
Your guess is as good as mine, and mine is that
there were always two.

Romberg

A maestro came to town when I was young
and gave me a lesson. I tackled Beethoven,
his third cello sonata, but the maestro stopped me,
warning that I was too young to perform
such great music. And, with hindsight, he was right:
even Dirty Harry said you have to know
your limitations.

The maestro told me to practise Romberg:
one of his concertos. They were good for technique,
said the maestro, if nothing else.
So I followed his advice, but it was hard
to find a Romberg concerto in the shops;
when I did, I practised it diligently,
negotiating the scales and arpeggios
as though ticking off items
on a shopping list.

Romberg, the greatest cellist of his day,
made some useful innovations — extending
the fingerboard, even simplifying clefs —
but he was no composer. Still,
when his friend Beethoven offered
to write him a concerto, Romberg declined.
Don't worry, he said, I've written enough of them:
ten, to be precise.

Was Beethoven offended?
We will never know; instead, we can only listen
to his violin concerto and wonder
what might have been.

Death by Selfie

It's perfect for Instagram:
that ledge on a limestone sea-cliff
with the sun kissing the horizon;
there's a warning sign, and it's roped off,
but he's known as a risk-taker
and, besides, he's backpacking and must share
this moment with his friends back home.

Standing next to their Volvo, a family
are taking in the view from the safety
of the bitumen, the mother staring
at him, grabbing her daughter's wrist as he steps
over the rope.

With his left hand, he holds a tuft of grass
to keep his balance, and with his right
he holds his phone high above his head
to capture the audacity of the moment,
so that his friends can marvel at the sheer drop
below his new trainers. He takes one photo
then, for dramatic effect, throws his left arm
in the air and takes another; now it's done
and soon he will be back in town, ordering
Chinese takeaway.

His foot slips. Only a fraction, but enough
for him to shudder. He snatches at the remnants
of a smashed fossil, glinting like eggshell,
offering the faint chance of a fingerhold,
but his other foot slips and he falls over
backwards.

He knows there is no point struggling:
from now on, he must be more bird than man.
No panic, or sadness, though certainly not peace;
regret, yes, for his mother's grief;
wonder, too, for what his lost years might have brought,
and even for what he might discover
about himself, and the yawning universe,
in the endless milliseconds before
he is dashed on the rocks below.

Only a cricket pitch distant, the girl is turning away,
already bored by the view. He must not cry out;
he does not want her waking up in a cold sweat,
afflicted by this memory in old age.

A sunbeam strikes the fossil and it winks at him,
telling him there is nothing to fear,
its weary eyelid burdened with the wisdom
gained over the countless millennia
since its ancient host swam the warm oceans,
and he is calm now, this has happened before:
he is Icarus with an iPhone.

The Twenty-Seventh Floor

Somehow, this blowfly managed to survive
the roller doors that crushed its companions,
the perilous expanse of the marble foyer,
the lunchtime crush of the elevator
as it scaled twenty-seven floors, even
the receptionist and her lethal can of flyspray,
and now it is perched on my desk
like some insectivore Ulysses.

How did it achieve this stupendous feat?
Was it a stowaway in a graduate's lunchbox,
or did it hitch a ride on the shoulder
of some venerable executive?
And what caused it to venture to this distant,
monochrome land of whispers, where my desk
is wiped and the trash collected daily,
and the air-conditioning is always set
at twenty-one degrees?

What does it see through those compound eyes,
each with more than a thousand lenses?
Does it gaze out the window at the sapphire sea
and the distant ranges, longing to escape
from this disinfected kingdom?

I should slip it some mouldy cheese
from the kitchen, or some overripe fruit,
as a measure of my respect.

Disenfranchised

Caused directly or indirectly by;
resulting from or in connection with;
arising out of or in relation to;
or, perhaps, in respect of, which allows
for the broadest possible connection.

Fine print on the back of parking tickets
and dry-cleaning dockets, and commonly
found in product disclosure statements;
exclusion clauses in your home insurance
and the delivery terms I had to accept
when I last ordered takeaway
through a multinational.

Weasel words of little consequence
except to those trained to read invisible
ink and to understand the myriad
degrees of legal and factual causation,
who know precisely when to rely on the
contra proferentum rule or that of
strictissimus juris, and know they are
protected from us by the medieval
fortress of the common law.

We Are All Just Passing Through

Our roof leaked overnight, so this morning
I called our handyman and asked him
if he could fix it. Moments later
he texted, saying he was in hospital
and wouldn't be able to work again.

We have known him for years,
calling whenever we needed help.
He is quiet, reclusive even, though
always pleasant: when he arrived,
he would only chat briefly,
refuse the obligatory offer of tea
or coffee before starting work.
So we don't know much about him
except that he is divorced and lives alone,
has a daughter somewhere in America.

His text was typically devoid of details
(was it cancer, heart disease or some
rare degenerative condition?)
but even more devastating
for the lack of them, as if he believed
those details didn't matter.

Even as I was typing my responding
text, wondering whether I should offer
to help, or else ask for his address
so that we could send him a gift,
I was trying not to be distracted
by the leaking roof, and the ineluctable
fact that we would need to find
someone else to fix it.

On the Doncaster Bus

There is an unspoken understanding:
never make eye contact with
fellow travellers, let alone start
a conversation.

The bus into town takes roughly an hour,
depending on traffic. That's a long time
to stay occupied and not bother
anyone. To that end, we used to read broadsheets,
held them up like shields against our neighbours,
but now we use smart phones and EarPods.

Even though we went to primary school
together, the woman who gets on near the
milk bar will never sit next to me; instead,
she often chooses a seat next to an elderly
fellow with a tie pin, balancing
a lunch box on his lap.

There used to be apple orchards
on Doncaster Hill. Now there are apartments
with city views and occupants with
limitless aspirations.

A Guide to Local Planning Laws

There's so much potential with this block,
says the architect, and the builder nods.
You have to maximise the northern light
so you should build two storeys along the southern
boundary all the way to the back fence.
But what about our neighbours, you ask,
won't they object? They need the northern light
for their vegetable patch.

If they object they won't stand a chance,
says the architect, and again the builder nods.
Besides, he adds, they can always grow tomatoes
somewhere else. Don't forget how much you paid
for your block. and this is within the guidelines.
Put it this way, adds the builder, when your
neighbours sell up, the buyers will bulldoze their house
and build along their own southern boundary:
after all, this is the inner city.

You have only met your neighbours briefly;
they are an elderly couple and have
invited you over for cake and tea.
Still, you have four children and need the extra
space upstairs. especially if you want
to keep the pool.

Remember, says the architect, this is allowed
under the guidelines. And that is sufficient
comfort, because the guidelines have surely
been drafted to protect your neighbours.
You can still admire your reflection
when you shave, because you are still a decent
citizen: why else would you pay tax at the top
marginal rate and not claim any
speculative deductions?

Morning Commute

Whenever I take the train to work,
I snare a window seat and soon dissolve
into the novel I am reading, oblivious
to the passing parade of urban developments
and even those hapless commuters
babbling endlessly on their iPhones;
still, when the train passes Richmond station,
no matter how engrossed I may be
in the novel, I put it aside and gaze
at a patch of grass fringing the
entrance to the city tunnel before
the train burrows underground, as if,
for a moment, I fear this sunlit
glory will be lost to me forever:
perhaps not this day, but another,
and sooner than I expect.

Sarabande

It is a slow and stately Baroque dance,
suitable even for elderly couples,
with its perils hidden from the listener
like thin ice covered by fresh snow,
troubling even the great Casals,
given that it was written for five strings,
not four. Many years I tried to master it,
plagued by the ideal of perfection, contorting
my fingers for those fiendish quadruple stops
while sustaining the intricate counterpoint,
to no avail. Still, there were moments
when the clouds lifted and I caught
glimpses of Bach's heavenly vision,
and this sustained me. Faust offered his soul
for a moment of bliss; I did not strike a pact,
but if I had ever managed to traverse
those four long minutes from one end to another
with the grace of a tightrope walker
keeping balance over a gaping ravine,
I might have attained lasting happiness.
The Ayatollah died, the Iron Curtain fell,
and still I fixated on my intonation,
as if the troubles of the entire world
could be disposed of like a dormouse
caught between my thumb and index finger.
I should have heeded the fate of Archimedes,
who was so intent on drawing perfect circles
in imperfect sand that he paid no regard
to the solider who ran him through.

The General in his Labyrinth

Towards the end, Marquez puts it this way:
the General finally realised that the race
between his dreams and misfortunes was over,
and even though he had liberated
half a continent, still his misfortunes prevailed.
That may be how it feels for the great and good
upon sudden humiliation in battle,
or at the ballot box, or in the newspapers;
but for the rest of us, that realisation
settles softly, like sediment in cheap wine.

For decades, we may stir ourselves
with relentless ambition, but one day,
exhausted, we find absolute clarity.
It may happen when we least expect:
watching a sitcom, watering the garden,
or taking out the recycling bin.
At first, we may rail against the vision
and search the bathroom mirror for destiny;
only in time we may realise that wine
is best savoured when the dregs have settled.

Afterwards

Melting

The arctic wind had stripped the woods
above the urban hemline,
leaving clumps of bony twigs
pointing scornfully at winter's lovers.

Oblivious, they hatch dinosaur-egg
snowballs, paste them together,
affix the carrot nose then join hands
and admire their creation
in silent ceremony: snowman,
sentinel of the barren slopes,
witness to their declarations
of enduring love.

The blossoms, coaxed from their buds
by the benign breath of spring,
find a rotting carrot on the crinkled mat
of last year's leaves.

Three Days

There were three days between her last meal
and last breath: three days as long as seasons
while we sat beside her hospital bed,
waiting for her to leave.

Every morning, the nurse would open the curtains,
clear away her untouched dinner and, in its place,
as a pointless ritual, leave another breakfast tray
with toast and milk tea.

In the afternoon, the priest would drop by
and bless her, saying that her work was done,
that she could now depart. But she did not listen
or, if she did, she firmly disagreed:
shaking her head, curling her lip
while she clawed the bedsheets,
grasping the rope of life as it dangled
over the abyss.

And at night, when the ward was still,
we could hear the angels calling her
while she resisted, stopping her ears
to their sweet melody.

Cold Cuts

We followed strict instructions
on the order of service:
the readings, the hymns, the music
for reflection, even the flowers —
little was left to chance.
And for the wake, she had asked us
to book her local bowling club:
a post-war cream-brick relic
nestled on prime land
with a splendid view of the ranges.

All went according to her plans:
surely she would have been touched
to hear the congregation sing
Jerusalem, to hear the minister's
heartfelt words, to watch us stumble
over our eulogies. Until we reached the
bowling club. Because she hadn't given
instructions on the catering.

We had been told that she was
much loved by other members,
so we prepared bounteous
club sandwiches and the choicest
desserts for the trestles —
and there they largely stayed,
as members she had rolled with
for ten long years came in
from the greens, glanced across
at us, hesitated, then decided
not to join our dwindling band,
but instead collect their bags
and wander out to the carpark.

We should not have been so aggrieved:
after all, in heaven's waiting room,
perhaps this occasion was not
of much importance. And perhaps
she had long departed and the rituals
and even these cold cuts were only
ever intended for us, not for her.

Silverware

They faced each other across her dining
table as though about to play chess
and took it in turns to divide the family
silverware. First, he chose the serving
platter; next, she took the sugar bowl;
he paused, surveyed the tarnished
bundle between them, and took the salad tongs,
leaving her to prevaricate on her next move.

After dividing the real estate and the
furniture, they had expected this task
would be easy and had left it until last.
But the delay had invested even the dessert
spoons with heightened significance.
An antique dealer may not have
any interest in these leftovers,
but, for them, each remaining item
summoned its own unique memories.

Now she regretted losing the serving
platter; their mother had used it for countless
weekend gatherings. Without it, perhaps
memories of those occasions would swiftly
fade: she should make her next choice carefully.
Yet as she was deliberating on whether to
choose the ashtray or the cigarette box
(even though she didn't smoke),
he stood up and left without a word.

Perhaps he regretted passing up the sugar
bowl. Or else he figured that when this
sad and dwindling pile of trinkets
had been divided there may be
nothing else connecting them.

Reunion

Where else would you find a roomful of men
exactly fifty-two years old,
except for a clinical trial
or an odd social experiment?

Nametags are obligatory:
how else could we tell apart
the victim from his erstwhile tormentor?
Now both are hidden behind ample skinfolds
and prescription lenses, mumbling pleasantries,
even exchanging stockmarket tips.

I remind myself it's only one evening:
painless, and I can always leave early,
skip the bawdy speeches and the school song;
they are now strangers and I belong elsewhere,
even though we once walked the same carpet.
Still, I can't help but feel sympathy
for the football hero with the arthritic hip
and the alcoholic rower and, even worse,
the marble-eyed financial planner
who once dreamed of Hollywood.

And I know this evening will linger
like stale cigarette smoke, because my life
is measured in the five-year intervals
of these autumnal gatherings, at which
some leaves are crimson, some brown,
and others are resting on the forest floor.

Old Friends

Old friends are the best friends.
Only they can remind you of
the risks that you took when you were
young; only they can remind you of
your early triumphs; only they
share your offbeat sense of humour.
When you are with them, decades
fall away and you find yourself
back in your prime, when the world
was new, and strange, and awash with the
heady brew of desire and destiny.

But old friends are also the worst friends.
Only they can remind you of
your earliest fears; only they
can remind you of your worst mistakes;
only they know your pressure points and,
if they are so inclined, cause you
to buckle with the slightest touch.
Worse, as those decades fall away,
they see you not as you want to be seen,
perhaps not even as you are, but only
as you were and will forever be.

Assembly

He arrives early, finds a seat at the front
near some other grandparents,
with a perfect vantage of the children
bustling in from the playground,
stands reverently as the principal
leads off with the anthem, then watches
as she calls out the pupils of the week,
the finest of the next generation,
who shuffle on stage to collect their awards.

Congratulations, Emma, for mastering
the alphabet; Ava, for counting all the way
to fifty; William, for cleaning up
after art class; Noah, for asking great questions
in maths – great work Noah; Hannah, for raking
the vegetable patch; James, for spelling
locomotive; and Isabelle, for being
such a great friend to your friends.

Each name, each citation, is pronounced
with solemnity befitting an Anzac parade
and he looks around, puzzled, at the other
grandparents measuring off the stage
through their iPhones, feeling like Marco Polo
in the court of Kublai Khan. How could anyone
not be a friend to their friends? He tries
to recall the last time he received an award
or, if not an award, some form of
commendation but nothing comes to mind;
the past fifty years have been marked not by acclaim
but only service: even on his retirement
there was no gold watch, no rousing speech,
just severance pay.

And he wonders if this ceremony,
with these brief moments on stage, is fair
to the children holding up their precious
certificates and basking in the applause:
if this is what they can expect, then how
will they endure the waiting decades?
But there is no time for him to follow
these thoughts to their logical conclusion
because, just then, the principal calls up
his own grandson and, proud as ever,
he holds up his phone to catch the moment.

Daylight Saving

This morning, I awoke from benign dreams
to discover that I have lost an hour.
It wasn't as dramatic as the year
that I was late to the airport for a
domestic flight with a non-refundable
ticket, nor even the year that I missed
coffee with friends. And it has benefits:
tomorrow I will not be woken so early
by the magpies, and I can now look forward
to long sunlit evenings. Still, I have lost an hour
that I will never recover.

Even though it was stolen from me
when I was asleep, prised ever so gently
from my grasp; even though the thief
lingered briefly at my bedside, forever
a doting parent: still it is gone and I am
one hour closer to singing Auld Lang Syne
for the last time.

Park Bench

It's just a bench on a scrubby hillside
in a suburban dormitory:
no tourists or postcard views.
On one side, there's a housing estate,
typical seventies brown-brick
where there once were apple orchards;
on another, an artificial lake
swelled by stormwater run-off;
still, if you look straight ahead
there's a decent view of glinting rooftops
and, nestled in a cradle of distant ridgelines,
even a glimpse of the horizon
under a thumbprint of smog.

It's just a bench on a scrubby hillside.
I used to sit here when I was young,
seeking solitude in the gathering dusk,
wondering why distant streetlights twinkle
and why cut grass smells of summer
and where life would lead me.

It's just a bench on a scrubby hillside
and now I sit here again, forty years hence.
It's badly in need of repair:
the boards rotten, the bolts scabbed with rust;
soon, what is left of the horizon
will be obscured by an overgrown hedge –
but I am not here for the view.
Closing my eyes, I search for the lost child
who sat here all those years ago,
never expecting to return.

Deception

They say a mirror never deceives you,
unlike friends or family or lovers;
why, then, does it insist my hair is brown
when, in the barbershop, the cuttings
on the floor are clearly grey,
with strands of white? Maybe
it is just a trick of the lighting
because all the other evidence
suggests that I am still young,
not a frog in a pot of water
slowly coming to the boil.

Tipping Point

At first, they didn't bother me,
those clumps of algae in our pond:
after all, I could pull them out by the roots
whenever I fed the goldfish.

But they spread with the blessing of the summer sun,
tendrils trailing from the fountainhead
like bushranger beards, strangling the filter.
I drank iced tea to endure the heatwave,
while reading news about distant bushfires.

Now, when I tried to feed them, the fish
no longer rippled the surface with quicksilver tails;
instead they lingered in the lilies, or cruised
in lazy circles as if swimming through oil.
I stripped back more algae, while the filter
spluttered on like a smoker's ventricles.
And there was the mild scent — not unpleasant —
of seaweed abandoned by the tide.

One morning, a carcass floated to the surface
with eyes of sepulchral marble:
I scooped it out, buried it in
unconsecrated soil near the post box,
while hoping it had reached its natural term.
Then I drank more tea and waited
for the heatwave to end.

The next morning, all the other fish were
bobbling on the surface like harpooned whales,
with their dead eyes judging me
and the crows perched overhead.

First Light

He strains to remember the first moment
that he can safely call a memory
from the many incidents posturing on hind legs,
jostling for attention.

What, then, must it be? That night he lost contact
with his mother in a department store
and searched for her amongst that multitude
of unfamiliar faces? Or the morning
he was swamped by surf while cross-legged
on the sand? Or the afternoon
when the neighbour's dog drooled at him
with that rabid stare? The world has always
been his jungle, with tigers lurking
in the undergrowth.

But still, one image brings him solace,
slows his breath. It is the lamp
beside his childhood cot: strawberry enamel
with a flickering bulb, no brighter than
a solitary candle, casting a faint ring
of sunrise pink and keeping him safe
from the shadows.

Grey Nomad

They told him, with obvious regret,
that youth was wasted on the young,
so he resolved not to repeat their mistakes.
Instead of taking that dreary job
straight out of school, he drank moonshine
and smoked strange cigarettes,
danced until dawn on sawdust floors,
woke in unfamiliar beds, travelled the world
to find the perfect sunrise.

Indeed, this brought some contentment.
There were times he believed that if he had
keeled over, not taken another step,
his life would have been worthwhile,
if not complete.

He figured that middle age should stretch out
like a hammock in a shady hollow
between the vigour of youth
and the rigour of old age,
so he eventually took that office job
and spent decades in a fishbowl,
growing his superannuation
and counting the days until he escaped.

With an arthritic knee and rickety shoulder
he now ventures into freezing waters
with a borrowed longboard,
paddling beyond the breakwaters
while fearing rips and white pointers,
but is unable to catch a wave.

As the sun sets, and he is ready to give up,
a wave catches the tail of his board
and he springs to his feet.
For a moment, one fleeting moment,
he miraculously finds his balance
as the wave curls underneath
and he rides it to shore.

He has the insight of a prisoner before
a firing squad, and grasps that all the drugs
and the dancing and the revelry
and even the decades of boredom
are all improbably balanced upon each other,
that without them this could never have happened:
then the wave breaks and he topples over.

Coda

Awakening

It begins well before dawn,
before the birds flutter beside the fishpond
and the children are awake;
I am lying in bed, the streetlamp
sluicing gold dust through the lace curtains,
drugged, unable even to move my toes,
ruminating on a half-remembered dream –
or was it a nightmare? – my mind wrapped
in gauze bandages.

At first, it is barely audible above
my partner's breath and the stealthy fugue
of the heating ducts; then, as I listen
carefully, I catch that distant note,
subtle as the blood pulsing in my ears:
the song of the metropolis,
of the motorway, of the arterial roads,
of the side-streets and the cut-throughs,
as bleary-eyed commuters, listening to Adele
and Rihanna and talk-back radio, trickle in
from distant suburbs, rivulets feeding into streams,
and streams feeding into rivers. But as I lie there,
and the dream fades, and my mind settles slowly,
reluctantly, on the task list of the coming day,
and the streetlight is eclipsed by the pink hues of dawn,
and the birds begin their own antique song,
and there are footsteps in the hallway,
the note gains intensity, becomes a distinct hum, like
a dentist's drill through a closed door,
and then an open door, punctuated
with angry bursts of horn, the sharp staccato
of a motorbike, and now even the rattle of tram lines.

I tremble like a tuning fork:
the exact pitch has been struck
to jangle my eardrums, rattle my ossicles;
I wish that I lived in the country
at least a mile distant from any road
or even any neighbour, and for once
I could doze as I please; there is no escaping
this unwelcome assault — not earplugs, not double-glazing —
invading every corner of our home
like woodsmoke from the neighbours' chimney.
Yet I realise, begrudgingly, that it serves
its purpose, that the cacophony
is my clarion call, rousing me from bed
to confront the day.

But today, as the sun rises
and the birds sing and, in the kitchen,
the children scavenge for cereal,
there is no hum, not even that distant note.
Someone has thrown a blanket over the city
as heavy as blizzard snow, stifling it in its sleep.
I wonder if my ears are wax-clogged
or if old age has finally snared me in its trap,
until I remember that today, indeed,
is different: there is no work,
there is no play; instead, we must slumber
like an army of the dead.

Fresh Produce

I had a dream, which was not all a dream

Byron

A fight breaks out in the supermarket
and it's not where I had expected. Someone
coughs among the queue of hunter-gatherers waiting
for the toilet-paper delivery truck
but, apart from a murmur of derision,
the tension swiftly passes; someone else
pounces on the last dozen packets of pasta,
shovels them into his trolley in full view
of the woman waiting just behind him,
but she just shrugs and instead chooses basmati rice:
no, of all places, it's the fresh produce aisle,
even though there is no shortage of fruit
and vegetables. Leaning on her walking stick,
an old lady prods a peach with her bejewelled,
arthritic talon to check if it is ripe
then, obviously displeased, prods another
until a lady with a walking frame tells her
never to handle the fruit, causing the first
to wave her stick and resort to arcane
insults. Both aggrieved, they appeal
to a pimpled youth wearing latex gloves
and surgical mask, unpacking bananas.
I wander across to offer support,
as he is not long out of school and
untrained in the subtle art of mediation,
but then the toilet paper arrives and both women
lose all interest in fruit and join the queue
and, relieved, I hurry to the checkout.

Treasurer

How do we measure a human life:
is there some algorithm by which
we can weigh it against GDP,
or else some crude instrument that would
serve like makeshift kitchen scales —
one hundred lives on one side, evenly
balanced against who knows how many
dollars on the other? That is what
the treasurer is thinking as he watches
the health minister from a safe distance
across the broad, sanitised expanse
of the cabinet-room conference table.
But he cannot ask, because he cannot
formulate the question in any way
that will avoid raised eyebrows from
junior ministers, and he does not want
an indiscreet comment to be leaked
to news outlets, fuelling speculation that
he traded his beating heart for one of glass.
Instead, he sips herbal tea, reads a briefing paper
calling for stricter lockdown measures
and wonders how to refute it, knowing
that every day of lockdown means
thousands more lost jobs, and not knowing
how to fund those unemployed, and somehow
stuck in the numbers like a bicycle wheel
caught in a tram track. The rice cracker
he nibbles reminds him of communion wafer,
body of Christ — and for a moment he is kneeling
before the altar and seeking favour,
or is it forgiveness? (He never can tell.)
But no matter, the crumbs dissolve on his tongue
and as they dissolve the question

overwhelms him. This is not what he studied
at law school; this is not what he
trained for at the consulting firm;
this was not what he was expecting
from his political career. If only he held
a different portfolio.

Home Office

He does not miss the dreary commute
for an hour on an eight-lane freeway,
the bus shuddering so that he cannot read
but instead must survive on podcasts,
the knees of commuters next to him
so often splayed sideways because of
their overstuffed bags — that is,
when he is lucky enough to snare a seat;
and, if even he does miss it, perhaps it is only
for those moments in the evening
when he steps off the bus and ambles past
the broken streetlamp to his front door.

He does not miss the lunchtime walk
past the buskers playing panpipes
who remind him of his trip to Peru
so many years ago, the walk down the
graffitied laneway to his favourite
takeaway joint, where he waits in line
for chicken wings and chips;
he does not even miss the aroma of those wings,
the grease spots spreading on the paper bag
as he heads back to his office to savour them
at his desk while reading the news.

So much, perhaps, is unsurprising.
But what does surprise him is that
he does not miss the tearoom banter
or the meetings with his clients;
he does not miss his team members
asking for guidance. Human contact,
at least for him, is now overrated.

When he was young, not a weekend
went by without mindless celebration;
he was always surrounded by friends,
at least he called them friends; in time,
they drifted away with their wives
and children, and for years he was entirely
preoccupied with his work, and on weekends
he drove his own children to countless
parties and sporting events, but now his children
have left home, and his wife has left too,
for a life in the country with a retired dentist,
and he has eventually discovered that
he is entirely satisfied with his own company.

Is he depressed or somehow defective:
should he make an appointment with his doctor?
But what should he declare – that he is Major Tom,
that his marionette strings have been severed?
He does not want to confess this
because he can easily content himself
in his spare time by trimming the hedges,
reading crime thrillers, and watching
the football. Who is to say this
is not a life well-spent? And with perfect
broadband connection he can work all day
at his kitchen table and still maintain budget.

Constitutional

I live in an enclave of domesticated weathercocks.
Here, there are clipped hedges, not rainforests,
freshly-mown lawns instead of unkempt meadows,
and in place of plunging mountain ravines
there are concrete gutters choked with plastic.

Every morning, confined by unforgiving ordinance
to my suburb, I set off around the block
with dutifully-strapped surgical mask,
so that instead of the elusive scent of blossoms
I must make do with percolated-coffee breath.
Fleetingly, I remember that Hamlet,
though bounded in a nutshell,
counted himself the king of infinite space:
perhaps indeed the mind's eye can deceive,
but that requires hope, and how can there be hope
when the streets are empty, the shops shuttered
and the playgrounds deserted?

Still, when I pass a row of stunted elms
I can imagine a grand Parisian boulevard,
and the terracotta roof tiles of a modest bungalow
bring to mind the glories of the Alhambra;
the patch of dirt across the road brings visions
of splendid Saharan wastelands,
and the hillock beside the train line
reminds me of the vast slopes of Mont Blanc.

My wanderings lead me to an abandoned park
hemmed in on all sides by suburbia.
There, I take off my cap, lower my mask
to inhale the subantarctic breeze
and give thanks for all that remains,
while admiring the solitary oak
still yet to shed its leaves.

Acknowledgements

I am deeply grateful to David Musgrave of Puncher & Wattmann, for giving life to this collection. My heartfelt thanks also to Miranda Douglas for her beautiful cover design, Judith Beveridge and Peter Goldsworthy for their generous endorsements, and my agent Fiona Inglis for her unwavering support.

These poems were written on the lands of the Wurundjeri people of the Kulin Nation, and I pay my respects to Elders past and present.

I am indebted to all my friends and extended family for their love, support and encouragement. And, as always, I reserve my deepest gratitude for my wife Dinusha and our children, Oscar and Sylvie.

www.ingramcontent.com/pod-product-compliance
Lightning Source LLC
Chambersburg PA
CBHW030855090426
42737CB00009B/1240